GROW YOUR MIND

ASK
FOR
HELP

Written by Izzi Howell

Illustrated by David Broadbent

CRABTREE
PUBLISHING COMPANY

WWW.CRABTREEBOOKS.COM

CRABTREE
PUBLISHING COMPANY
WWW.CRABTREEBOOKS.COM

Author: Izzi Howell
Series designer: David Broadbent
Illustrator: David Broadbent
Editor: Crystal Sikkens
Proofreader: Melissa Boyce
Print coordinator: Katherine Berti

A trusted adult is a person (over 18 years old) in a child's life who makes them feel safe, comfortable, and supported. It might be a parent, teacher, family friend, social worker, or another adult.

Library and Archives Canada Cataloguing in Publication

Title: Ask for help / written by Izzi Howell ; illustrated by David Broadbent.
Names: Howell, Izzi, author. | Broadbent, David, 1977- illustrator.
Description: Series statement: Grow your mind | Includes index. | First published in Great Britain in 2020 by the Watts Publishing Group.
Identifiers: Canadiana (print) 20200221558 | Canadiana (ebook) 20200221698 | ISBN 9780778781653 (hardcover) | ISBN 9780778781738 (softcover) | ISBN 9781427125910 (HTML)
Subjects: LCSH: Help-seeking behavior—Juvenile literature. | LCSH: Helping behavior in children—Juvenile literature. | LCSH: Helping behavior—Juvenile literature.
Classification: LCC HM1141 .H69 2021 | DDC j158.3—dc23

Library of Congress Cataloging-in-Publication Data

Names: Howell, Izzi, author. | Broadbent, David, 1977- illustrator.
Title: Ask for help / written by Izzi Howell ; illustrated by David Broadbent.
Description: New York : Crabtree Publishing Company, 2021. | Series: Grow your mind | Includes index.
Identifiers: LCCN 2020014612 (print) | LCCN 2020014613 (ebook) | ISBN 9780778781653 (hardcover) | ISBN 9780778781738 (paperback) | ISBN 9781427125910 (ebook)
Subjects: LCSH: Help-seeking behavior--Juvenile literature. | Helping behavior in children--Juvenile literature.
Classification: LCC HM1141 .H69 2021 (print) | LCC HM1141 (ebook) | DDC 158.3--dc23
LC record available at https://lccn.loc.gov/2020014612
LC ebook record available at https://lccn.loc.gov/2020014613

Crabtree Publishing Company
www.crabtreebooks.com   1-800-387-7650
Published by Crabtree Publishing Company in 2021

Published in Canada
Crabtree Publishing
616 Welland Ave.
St. Catharines, Ontario
L2M 5V6

Published in the United States
Crabtree Publishing
347 Fifth Ave.
Suite 1402-145
New York, NY 10116

Printed in the U.S.A./082020/CG20200601

First published in Great Britain in 2020 by The Watts Publishing Group Copyright © The Watts Publishing Group 2020

CONTENTS

Help and mindsets

When you're working on something difficult or new, you sometimes get to a point where you are stuck and need help. What goes through your mind when this happens?

I don't understand, but I don't want anyone to know I need help!

I'm going to ask for help so that I can understand this better!

The first idea comes from **fixed-mindset** thinking. This is the idea that your intelligence is fixed and can't be changed. People who think with a fixed mindset are often scared to ask for help. They think asking for help is a sign of failure.

The second idea comes from **growth-mindset** thinking. This is the idea that you can grow and develop your intelligence through effort and hard work. People who think with a growth mindset know that asking questions and getting help are great ways to learn and help your brain grow.

No one is born with the ability to do everything. You have the power to change your brain and help it to grow stronger and learn more.

Inside your brain are billions of **neurons** that are connected to each other. They carry information around your brain and to and from the rest of your body. What you think and do strengthens these neurons and helps create new ones.

Asking for help, whether it's asking a question, asking for someone to repeat instructions, or asking for advice, helps create new connections between neurons. It's a great way to check that you are learning properly, and that you are on the right path to a stronger, happier brain!

Everyone needs help

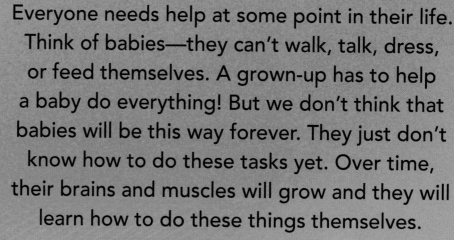

Everyone needs help at some point in their life. Think of babies—they can't walk, talk, dress, or feed themselves. A grown-up has to help a baby do everything! But we don't think that babies will be this way forever. They just don't know how to do these tasks yet. Over time, their brains and muscles will grow and they will learn how to do these things themselves.

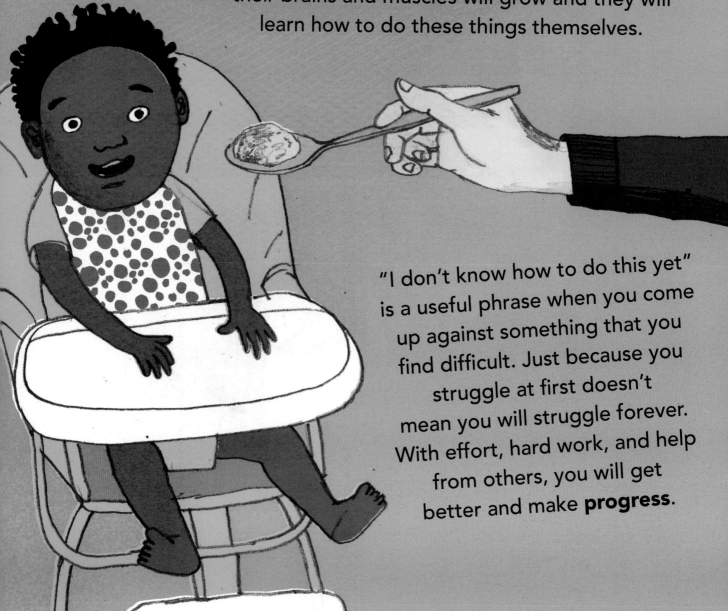

"I don't know how to do this yet" is a useful phrase when you come up against something that you find difficult. Just because you struggle at first doesn't mean you will struggle forever. With effort, hard work, and help from others, you will get better and make **progress**.

Amir

My friends and I love to go out on
our skateboards. I know how to do
a few tricks that are really fun!

One day, my friend Ella showed me a new trick she had learned
from her sister. You jump in the air, and the board flips all the
way around before you land on it! I had no idea how to do the
trick, but I gave it a try. It didn't work and I fell on the ground.

I didn't want to ask Ella how she did it because I felt
embarrassed. Then I saw her explaining it to someone else,
and I listened. She gave some really good tips.

I practiced the trick a few more times,
doing what Ella said, and I finally got it!

Problems on the mind

When something is difficult,
it can feel overwhelming, like a giant black cloud
weighing down on you. It could be something that you
are struggling with at school, a problem with your friends,
or something else that you are worried about.

One of the best ways to make a change is by asking for help.
Just this simple action can help to lift the black cloud
and make you feel better.

And then, of course, getting the help—whether it's
advice about a friend or help with schoolwork—is a
great step toward solving the problem!

When you're feeling stressed about a problem, it's sometimes hard to think clearly about a solution. It can help to take a break before asking for help or trying to solve the problem yourself.

Here are some ways to snap out of a stressful moment!

★ **Get moving by doing some exercise.**

★ **Think about your favorite place or a happy memory.**

★ **Close your eyes and take some deep breaths.**

★ **Do something with your hands, like making a model from clay.**

★ **Have a healthy snack or a glass of water.**

What other ideas can you think of?

Be brave

Some people feel embarrassed when they need help. This comes from fixed-mindset thinking. They believe they won't be seen as smart if they ask for help.

But this isn't true! Asking questions is a strength. It's one of the best ways to help your brain grow strong and learn new things. It's important to be brave and ask for help, even if you feel scared. Try to ignore these negative feelings and focus on how things are going to be easier with help.

Sometimes the hardest part of asking for help is choosing the right words. It can be easier to be brave when you don't have to worry about what you are going to say!

Why not make a poster to hang up in your classroom with some phrases that people can use when asking for help? Then, when you need to ask for help, you can quickly choose one of the phrases and get the help you need!

Can I ask you a question about…?

Could you repeat the part about…?

I'm confused about…Can you help me?

Can we go over…again?

I'm struggling with…What should I do?

What does…mean?

How do I…?

How can I **improve** my learning?

Speaking Up

Try not to feel embarrassed about asking for help. It's a normal, everyday part of life and it helps your brain grow stronger!

Sharing your experiences of asking for help can inspire others to do the same. It's often easier to be brave and ask for help after hearing about other people who did the same thing.

Why not talk to your friends and family about times that you have asked for help? How did you know you needed help? Who did you ask for help and how did they help you? This will help your friends and family think about areas in which they need help, and build up the courage to ask for it.

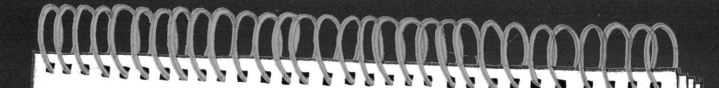

Over time, it can be easy to forget how other people have helped us achieve our goals. Why not keep track of these moments in a journal?

In the journal, write down things that people have told you in order to help you. They could be pieces of information, such as the fact that names, countries, and days of the week all begin with capital letters. They could also be words of advice. For example, "If you can't say anything nice, don't say anything at all!"

Make sure you write down the name of each person who helped you and what they taught you.

No silly questions

When you need help, you might worry that your question is silly or that people might laugh at you. It's important to remember that there are no silly questions when you are learning. Your brain knows what it needs to ask to learn more!

The only silly questions are the ones that you don't ask. These are silly because you are missing out on a chance to learn.

You may even find that other people have the same "silly" question as you. So by speaking up and being brave, you are helping others as well.

Prisha

Yesterday in science class, we were learning about insects.
Suddenly, a question popped into my mind—do butterflies
have teeth? I immediately felt like it was a silly question,
but I really wanted to know the answer.

So I put up my hand and asked the teacher.
A few people giggled, but the teacher stopped them
and said it was a really good question.

She explained about the proboscis, which is a tube that
butterflies use to suck up nectar and water. Then she taught
us about ant and beetle mandibles, which are kind of like teeth.

Even though I was scared to ask my question
at first, it ended up starting a really
interesting conversation.

Now I know a lot more about insects!

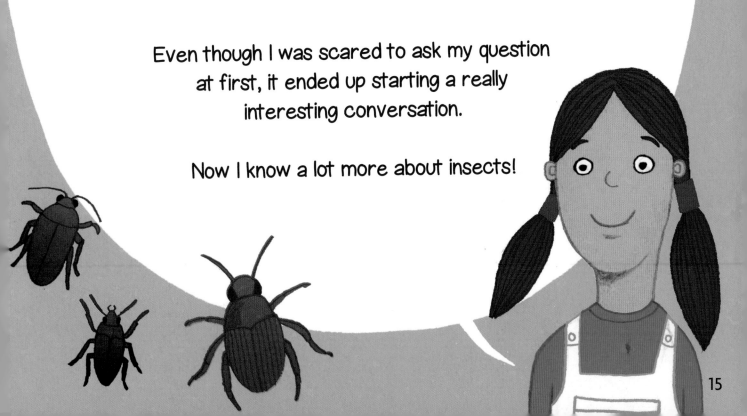

who can help?

Now that you're feeling ready to ask for help, who should you ask? There are a lot of people around you who can help, such as family members and other trusted adults. At school, you can ask your teacher or other people in your class.

If you get lost or have a problem away from home or school, you can ask a store employee or a police officer for help. If you get lost, stay where you are and don't go anywhere with a stranger.

You might be surprised who can help you. Your friends and family can help with personal problems, but they can also help with school problems. You can also go to your teacher or principal with any problems you're having at home or with your friends.

Patricia

Last week at school, we were learning about fractions. I seemed to understand it during class, but when I got home and started my homework, I felt really confused! I didn't know who to ask for help, since I was at home and couldn't ask my teacher. My mom and dad were busy, so I didn't want to bother them either.

Then my older sister noticed that I looked confused. She asked me if I needed any help. At first, I didn't want to bother her, but I knew I needed some help.

She remembered doing fractions when she was in my grade, so we worked on a few questions together. Working on my homework with my sister really helped me to understand fractions better. This week, I've been able to move on to harder fraction questions!

Helping others

Helping other people is a great way to boost your own brain. Explaining things to someone else gives you a great chance to practice thinking about them yourself, and it strengthens the connections between your neurons. It can also help the information to stick in your brain so you remember things better.

You might find that the other person asks you questions that you don't know the answer to. This is an opportunity for both of you to learn more and discover new information!

Why not make a help board for your classroom?

Ask everyone in the class to write down three things they feel they understand well and can help other people with. They could be things like multiplication tables, volcanoes, or even doing a cartwheel.

When someone needs help with something, they can look at the board to find a person who can help them.

If someone needs help with something that isn't listed on the board, they could add it to the "help wanted" section. Others can check this section to see if there is something they can help with.

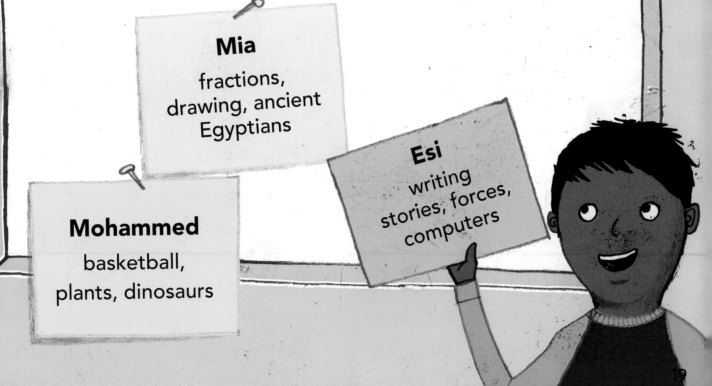

Mia
fractions, drawing, ancient Egyptians

Esi
writing stories, forces, computers

Mohammed
basketball, plants, dinosaurs

BUILDING TRUST

Asking for help and helping others are good ways to build strong relationships with other people. Going to someone for help shows that you trust them. Trust is very important in relationships.

Offering your help to someone who is having a hard time is also a good way to strengthen relationships. Giving and asking for help builds trust and lasting friendships with others.

Ethan

Last term, my family moved and I had to go to a new school. The first week was really hard because I didn't know anyone. My new class was working on a topic about forces, which we hadn't studied yet at my old school.

I didn't know anyone in my class yet so I felt scared to ask for help. One day, I was really confused about our lesson on friction, so I decided to ask the person sitting next to me for help.

He explained friction really well! After that, we started talking more and more, and playing together at recess. I even helped him learn how to dunk a basketball! Yesterday, he invited me to his birthday party.

Now I'm feeling much happier at school, and I'm doing well in our forces lessons!

TEAM POWER

Working with other people and sharing thoughts leads to creativity and new ideas.

Think of people like puzzle pieces.

Everyone's piece is slightly different, because of their own special ideas and skills.

All of these different pieces fit together to complete the puzzle.

See the power of teamwork by trying these activities and games with your friends. The combination of different skills, ideas, and points of view will come together to create something wonderful and original.

★ **Improvise** a short scene. First, decide on a setting and characters, and then see where you end up.

★ Work together to solve a challenge, such as building the tallest structure you can from newspaper. Or why not try building a structure to protect an egg when it is dropped from a certain height?

★ Write or tell a story together. Each person adds one sentence to the story at a time. What happens in the story?

Accepting feedback

When you ask for help, you have to be ready to listen to what other people think. Someone might say something negative that you don't want to hear. You might feel like ignoring this **feedback**, but if you do, you might miss out on some important help!

If you ask for help and someone gives you feedback that makes you feel bad, first take a deep breath and distract yourself with a positive thought, such as a pet, your favorite song, or a funny memory.

Then, look at the feedback from a positive point of view. How is this person trying to help? You might need to ask them to be more **specific** or give other examples (see page 26) if they aren't being clear.

Tyler

Yesterday, I was drawing a picture at school. It was a scene in the country with cows and trees. I was almost done, but I wasn't very happy with the drawing. Something didn't look right to me.

I asked my friend Ellie what she thought of it. I could tell right away that she didn't think it was very good either. She scrunched up her face and said, "It's a bit messy. What are those black-and-white things?"

At first, I felt disappointed in myself because I didn't do a very good drawing. But then I thought in a positive way about what Ellie said. I realized she was right. The cows were the problem.

I asked Ellie if she had any advice. She told me about a YouTube channel that gave a lot of good drawing tips. I watched one video about drawing animals and it gave me some great ideas on how to improve my cows!

As I was finishing my picture, Ellie looked over my shoulder and said the cows looked really good! She was right. The help from the video that she recommended made the drawing much better. At first, it was hard to hear Ellie's feedback, but I'm glad I asked her for help and listened.

SHARING OPINIONS

When you give **constructive** feedback to other people, it's important to give clear examples of what you think could be better. Don't just focus on the things that are wrong, suggest some ways they can improve.

Here are some useful phrases that you can use when giving other people feedback.

It would be even better if...

Why not try...?

I think that doing...would work well.

How about...?

Is there a more powerful word that you could use?

Have you double-checked it?

I like it when you use...

Have you thought about...?

It's also important to be kind. You could start by telling them what is working well, and then explain what needs some extra work. If you have some ideas about how to make it better, offer to help them fix it!

It can be useful to think of feedback as a sandwich. Positive comments are the bread and the constructive comment is the filling.

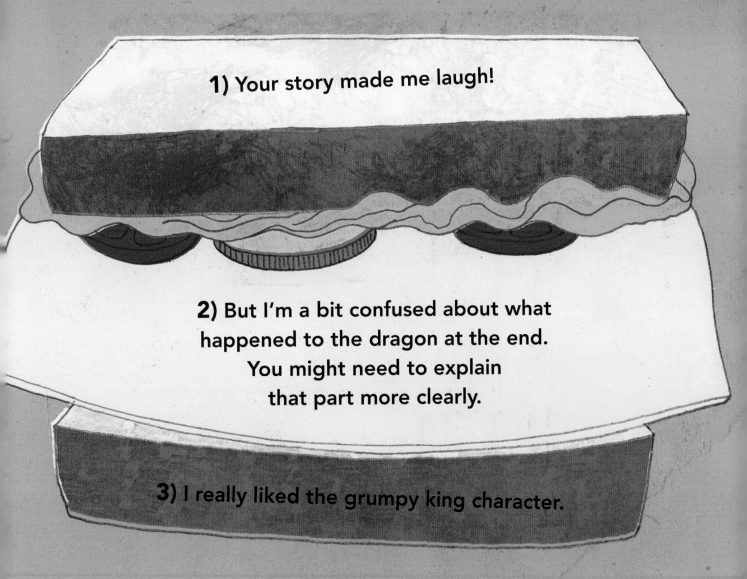

1) Your story made me laugh!

2) But I'm a bit confused about what happened to the dragon at the end. You might need to explain that part more clearly.

3) I really liked the grumpy king character.

Next time someone asks for your opinion, remember the sandwich when giving them feedback!

Helping yourself

Asking other people for help is a great way to learn and strengthen your brain. However, there will be times when there isn't anyone there to help you. So it's a good idea to learn how to solve your own problems, when you can. You often know more than you think. You might even know the solution without realizing it!

★ When you're feeling stuck with your schoolwork and need some help, try following this checklist to see if you can solve the problem yourself.

★ **What do I already know about this topic?**
You could draw a **mind map** to jog your memory.

★ **What can I use to help me?**
Try using resources such as a dictionary, a learning wall, cubes, or a number line to help.

★ **What is making this work difficult?**
Are you missing information because you've forgotten it, or is it something that you haven't learned yet?

★ **Look at a similar question or exercise that you've done before. How did you work out the answer?**
Think how you could use a similar strategy for this question.

★ **Do you have time to take a short break or move on to another question?**
Sometimes taking a break can help you develop new ideas. You might just come up with the solution while you are thinking about something else!

KEEP ASKING FOR HELP!

Read through this book's tips any
time you need a quick reminder!

Asking questions and getting help is a great
way to learn and help your brain grow.

When you are faced with something you
find difficult, just say to yourself, "I don't
know how to do this yet, but I can learn."

Asking for and getting help will make you feel better about your problems.

Be brave! Asking for help is a strength, so don't be afraid to speak up.

Sharing your experiences of asking for help will
inspire others to do the same, so don't be shy.

There are no silly questions! The only silly
questions are the ones you don't ask.

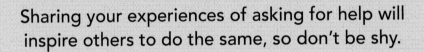

Your friends, family, teachers, and classmates can
help you with many different types of problems.

Helping other people is a great way to boost your own brain!

Asking for and offering help can build
strong relationships with other people.

Be prepared for other people's feedback—you may not
like it at first, but remember, they are trying to help!

When giving feedback to other people, it is important to
give clear examples of things they can make better.

Sometimes, you hold the answer to your own problem,
so trust your instincts and find a solution yourself!

Glossary

constructive   Describes advice that is useful and designed to help

feedback   Giving your opinion on something

fixed mindset   If you are using a fixed mindset, you believe that your intelligence is fixed and can't be changed

growth mindset   If you are using a growth mindset, you believe that your intelligence is always changing because your brain can grow stronger

improve   To get better

improvise   To speak or perform without preparing ahead of time

mind map   A diagram with lines and circles for organizing information so that it is easier to remember

neurons   Cells in your brain that pass information back and forth to each other

progress   Developing and improving your skills or knowledge

specific   Clear, with a lot of details or examples

Index

Notes for adults

The concept of a "growth mindset" was developed by psychologist Carol Dweck, and is used to describe a way in which effective learners view themselves as being on a constant journey to develop their intelligence. This is supported by studies showing how our brains continue to develop throughout our lives, rather than intelligence and ability being static.

Responding with a growth mindset means being eager to learn more and seeing that making mistakes and getting feedback about how to improve are important parts of that journey.

A growth mindset is at one end of a continuum, and learners move between this and a "fixed mindset"—which is based on the belief that you're either smart or you're not.

A fixed mindset is unhelpful because it can make learners feel they need to "prove" rather than develop their intelligence. They may avoid challenges, not wanting to risk failing at anything, and this reluctance to make mistakes—and learn from them—can negatively affect the learning process.

Help children develop a growth mindset by:

• Giving specific positive feedback on their learning efforts, such as "Well done, you've been practicing…" rather than non-specific praise, such as "Good effort" or comments such as "Smart girl/boy!" that can encourage fixed-mindset thinking.

• Sharing times when you have had to persevere with learning something new and what helped you succeed.

• Encouraging them to keep a learning journal, where they can explore what they learn from new challenges and experiences.

• Reminding them that asking for help is a strength, and encouraging them to offer help to others.